Ten Poems
from York

ex libris

Candlestick Press

Published by:
Candlestick Press,
Diversity House, 72 Nottingham Road, Arnold, Nottingham NG5 6LF
www.candlestickpress.co.uk

Design and typesetting by Craig Twigg

Printed by Bayliss Printing Company Ltd of Worksop, UK

Selection and Introduction © Ian McMillan, 2023

Cover illustration © James Green, 2023
http://jamesgreenprintworks.blogspot.com/

Candlestick Press monogram © Barbara Shaw, 2008

© Candlestick Press, 2023

ISBN 978 1 913627 27 0

Acknowledgements

The poems in this pamphlet are reprinted from the following books, all by
permission of the publishers listed unless stated otherwise. Every effort has been
made to trace the copyright holders of the poems published in this book. The
editor and publisher apologise if any material has been included without
permission, or without the appropriate acknowledgement, and would be glad to
be told of anyone who has not been consulted.

Thanks are due to all the copyright holders cited below for their kind permission.

Maura Dooley, *Life Under Water* (Bloodaxe Books, 2008) www.bloodaxebooks.
com. Helen Dunmore, *Counting Backwards: Poems 1975-2017* (Bloodaxe Books,
2019) www.bloodaxebooks.com. David Harmer, *Disturbed Ground* (Littlewood
Press, 1987) by permission of PLS Clear – Macmillan Press. Geoff Hattersley,
Harmonica (Wrecking Ball Press, 2006). Zaffar Kunial, *England's Green* (Faber
& Faber, 2022). Harold Massingham, *Frost-Gods* (Macmillan, 1971). Ian
McMillan, poem first appeared in this pamphlet. Pete Morgan, *A Winter Visitor*
(Martin Secker and Warburg, 1983) by kind permission of David Higham
Associates. Genny Rahtz, *Sky Burial* (Flux Gallery Press, 2010).

All permissions cleared courtesy of Dr Suzanne Fairless-Aitken
c/o Swift Permissions swiftpermissions@gmail.com

Where poets are no longer living, their dates are given.

Contents

Introduction

I know, I know: just ten poems to represent the whole of a county that is so big it only just fits on the map. Let's face it, Yorkshire is so big it only just fits into England, so how can ten poems do it justice?

I did try, gentle reader. I took my flat cap off and stood in the Candlestick Press offices and asked them if they could make a new publishing imprint called Candelabra just to bring out a book called 1000 Yorkshire Poems. They said they'd think about it so meanwhile here's ten Yorkshire poems old and new to keep you going.

The poems wander widely over time and space and there's also in some cases the gorgeous mouth music of the Yorkshire dialect, tha knows. Here is Yorkshire rendered in language, chiselled into lines and formed into stanzas. If poetry is the way we wished we spoke all the time, then here are ten voices to delight the ear. Ten poems, ten Yorkshires. Now there's a Sunday dinnertime idea: a poem in every Yorkshire, floating in the gravy!

Ian McMillan

The Spinner's Final Over

Every now and then I'll meet him
swaggering along this lane,
we'll exchange the time of day.

He asks if I am still the slowest
bowler Yorkshire knew.

Then perhaps I'll scratch a pattern
on this sun-scoured wall,
demonstrate a special lob
and just where to place the man.

Then my eight-legged hands
feel again the grip that wrapped
its sticky thread around his bat
a thousand times.

He walks away and I
can see him dying in the sun.

David Harmer

The Tarn

Still as the water is
the wind draws on it in iron

this is the purple country, the border
where we threw ourselves down
onto the heather.

Even the lapwing knows how to pretend.
She runs with her broken wing
to hide the fact of her young.

A cold small rain spatters the tarn
the wind writes on the dark water.

Helen Dunmore (1952 – 2017)

The 1984 Perspective
the enemy within (Margaret Thatcher, Orgreave)

Spoil. Slag, packed like sand dunes
all the way down the line to the coast
where coal, washed up on the beach,
handsome and useful, is scavenged
for a little warmth in a long winter.

Meltdown. Rolling stock, gone to Japan
for cars. Meltdown. The blur when
you can't tell who is moving: them or us.

Think of it now and what you see is not
the whole story but the seam of something
precious gone underground, a darkly silver trail
glistening as it vanishes. That's the point.

Maura Dooley

Hull

You may watch
How the River Hull
Slides her barges leeward
To the Humber
And shows these empty pods
A wedge of shadow
Sunk beneath their bows.

And the paddle steamer
With the red and black funnel
Still rides her half-circle
Round sandbanks to New Holland
To return, for a follower
Of her passage,
Abstracts of all her movements.

These routine passages of the eye
Belong to waterways
Whose tides leave their bloom
To silt the docks
And whose remnants of full use
Are warehoused
In semi-shrouded lots
On museum streets.

As yet there are no picture-postcards
Of these sights,
No more arranged to be visited
Than the old men
Who may be photographed
When they lie asleep,
Or the groups of boys
Seen fishing from the path
Of warehouse yards.

So attend this subdued city
Providing for its livelihood
Not its looks,
And keep what you find secret
From all obliterating praise.

Genny Rahtz

Winter in Wensleydale

Winter starts – with viking-skirmishes,
Rapid scoutings of squally north-east rain,

Marauds through Middle Wensleydale
With sleet like Arctic acids

Scarring mat-grass and becks from Masham to Askrigg,
Pittering Semmerwater till it simmers;

Or fourteenth-century north-easterlies
Jostle wet shrubbery, whine through Jervaulx Abbey's bones,

Pelting its frosty-silver masonry
With hail.
            Then snow, sheep-grey, a graceful

Fluff at first, falls on fells
Till cairn is snowman, moor-mound's

Moby Dick, and tussock-moss
Is thin dale-tundra. Then, thickening,

Like Christmas-crystals in a shaken glass,
A white sahara-storm, a lunar system

On the move, its smithereens gusting westward,
Winter rages to Upper Wensleydale,

Where sheep tinkle or perish
In bleak freezings, blizzardous drifts, and farms

Are like iced-up, isolated Arctic tents –
Secured by logics,

The dale-brain of generations
Bequeathed like heirlooms,

A stone stronghold-ing build,
An enduring commonsense of tiny windows.

Harold Massingham (1932 – 2011)

Inkling and Font

My baby's fingertip were *dusted*
that morning *in Yorkshire fog*
and his ears in poetry too

no font's liquid
but cloud's and earth's, suspended.
And composed, lifted quiet.

Zaffar Kunial

The Penistone Line

It can't be true that every day is just
a waste of breath: How this morning we heaved
ourselves from sleep and into the dull city,
heaved ourselves speechlessly up the steep hill
for no purpose; how a train conductor
is only now sauntering down the aisle
to say the train may be delayed for hours;
how this fact hurts, and how observation
can; how I might say he is a semi-
shaven gorilla, somehow forced into
the uniform – but won't. This is Barnsley,
glamorous Barnsley, the town I threw up in.
I look at my watch. You ask me to please
stop looking at my watch. *It's little things...*

That count, in the end. Like this fine view: grey
sky, grey buildings, grey people moving in
grey groups greyly. There are no fields full of
sheep, nor any other facts worth noting.
That's a fact. That's a certainty. But that
the whole thing should amount only to this!
I value friendship, love, kindness, all that
Happy Valley sort of stuff. Money – money
doesn't even come into it, and yet
if you and I argue ever, it's *that*
at the heart of it. I ask if you'd like
a cigarette, you don't reply. I light
one myself. Here's one fact: My eyes are bright
exploding suns. Yes. I look at my watch.

Geoff Hattersley

Coom, stop at yam to-neet, Bob

"Coom, stop at yam to-neet, Bob,
    Dean't gan oot onnywhere:
Thoo gets thisel t' leeast vex'd, lad,
    When thou sits i' t' awd airm-chair.

"There's Keat an' Dick beath want thee
    To stop an' tell a teale:
Tak little Keatie o' thy knee,
    An' Dick 'll sit on t' steal.

"Let's have a happy neet, Bob,
    Tell all t' teales thoo can tell;
For givin' pleeasure to the bairns
    Will dea thee good thisel.

"I knaw it's sea wi' me, Bob,
    For oft when I've been sad,
I've laik'd an' laugh'd wi' them, mon,
    Untel my heart's felt glad.

"An' sing that laatle sang, Bob,
    Thoo used to sing to me,
When oft we sat at t' river saade,
    Under t' awd willow tree.

"What happy taames them was, Bob,
    Thoo niver left me then
To gan to t' yal-hoose neet be neet
    Amang all t' drunken men.

"I does my best for thoo, Bob,
    An' thoo sud dea t' seame for me:
Just think what things thoo promised me
    Asaade t' awd willow tree!"

"I prithee say nea mair, lass,
    I see I ain't dean reet;
I'll think of all thoo's said to me,
    An' stop at yam to-neet.

"I'll try to lead a better life –
    I will, an' that thoo'll see!
Fra this taame fo'th I'll spend my neets
    At yam, wi' t' bairns an' thee!"

Florence Tweddell (1824 – 1899)

A Week of Yorkshire Haiku

Monday

Accidentally
Border-crossed ter Lankasheer
An felt reyt badly

Tuesday

Hung weshin on't line.
My vest flew off an slapped mi:
A soft white eclipse.

Wednesday

Early closin day
For the sky this midwinter.
Pull mi muffler tight.

Thursday

Call it dialect
If you must. Call it flyin
Moor like. Words air-kissed.

Friday

In the bus shelter
Two tight-lipped blokes not speykin
But sayin plenty.

Saturday

A Yorkshire sunset:
An old sleck fire's last embers.
A glowin flat cap.

Sunday

The egg. The flour.
The milk. The bowl. The old fork.
Then the transcendence.

Ian McMillan

Names

In the midst of nothing
There are names –

Nun Slack
Where religion grips
In earthworks and in tumuli.

Three Lords' Stones
Where no lords prosper.

Pye Rigg End
Where nothing ends
But rather is the rain's beginning.

Pete Morgan